Bridging K to 1

W9-AAU-618

Summer SPLASH

LEARNING ACTIVITIES

Brighter Child®
An imprint of Carson-Dellosa Publishing LLC
Greensboro, North Carolina

Brighter Child®
An imprint of Carson-Dellosa Publishing LLC
P.O. Box 35665
Greensboro, NC 27425 USA

© 2012 Carson-Dellosa Publishing LLC. Except as permitted under the United States
Copyright Act, no part of this publication may be reproduced, stored, or distributed in
any form or by any means (mechanically, electronically, recording, etc.) without the
prior written consent of Carson-Dellosa Publishing LLC. Brighter Child® is an imprint of
Carson-Dellosa Publishing LLC.

Printed in the USA • All rights reserved.   ISBN 978-1-60996-967-7

01-051121151

Table of Contents

Making the Most of
Summer Splash Learning Activities

This resource contains a myriad of fun and challenging reading and math activities. The reading pages provide practice in reading comprehension, grammar, phonics, and writing. The math pages review skills taught in kindergarten, such as patterning, counting, shapes, and numbers.

Most of the activities in the book are designed so that your child can work independently. However, your child will enjoy the activities much more if you work alongside him or her. Make sure to let your child know that this is not a workbook with tests, but a book of fun activities that you can do together. The book is divided into 10 weeks, with eight activity pages per week. Feel free to choose how many per day and in which order you do the activities, but complete the weeks in sequence, since activities become increasingly challenging as the book progresses.

Summer Splash Learning Activities provides an important link between your child's kindergarten and first-grade school years. It reviews what your child learned in kindergarten, providing the confidence and skills that he or she needs for the coming fall. The activities in this book will help your child successfully bridge the gap between kindergarten and first grade by reviewing and reinforcing the important and essential skills for his or her continued academic success. These activities are designed to

- review skills in math, reading, and language arts that your child learned the previous year.

- give you an opportunity to monitor your child's skills in various areas.

- offer you a chance to spend special time with your child.

- enable your child to continue routine daily learning activities.

- give you a chance to praise your child's efforts.

- demonstrate to your child that you value lifetime learning.

- make you an active and important part of your child's educational development.

Getting Started

In order for your child to get the most from the activities in this resource, use these helpful tips to make these learning experiences interesting and, most of all, fun!

- Set aside a time each day for completing the activities. Make it a time when your child will be most ready to learn, and make it a routine.
- Provide a pleasant, quiet place to work. This means no TV in your child's work area. Also, make sure there is a sufficient light source.
- Review in advance the activity page(s) your child will complete that session. This way, you will be able to familiarize yourself with the lesson.
- Have your child read the directions aloud beforehand to make sure he or she understands the activity. Instructions are written for the child, but he or she may need your help reading and/or understanding them.
- Let your child help choose which activity he or she would like to complete that day.
- Praise all your child's work. It's the effort, not necessarily the end result, that counts most.

No one knows better than you how your child learns best, so use this book to enhance the way you already work with him or her. Use every opportunity possible as a learning experience, whether making a trip through the grocery store or riding in the car. Pose problems and let your child figure out how to solve them, asking questions such as *Which route should we take to the park? What could we use to make a plant grow straight?* or *How high should we hang this shelf?* Also, respond excitedly to discoveries your child makes throughout the day with comments such as *That rock is really unique! I wonder how long it took the spider to spin that web;* or *You spent your money wisely.* In this way, you will encourage and motivate your child to learn throughout the day and for the rest of his or her life, providing the confidence and self-esteem he or she needs for continued academic success.

Everyday Learning Activities

Use these simple educational activities to keep your child's mind engaged and active during the summer months and all year long!

- Ask your child to make a schedule of events for the day, in the order in which they will take place. Ask him or her to prioritize the list and number the events.

- On a neighborhood walk or while driving in the car, encourage your child to read all the street signs and numbers.

- Read with your child each day. Encourage your child to retell the story to you. Then, have him or her make up original adventures for the story characters or write an additional chapter.

- Have your child write down important dates such as family birthdays, important trips or outings, or holidays. Be sure your child capitalizes the name of the month and week and uses a comma between the day and year.

- During a visit to the park or playground, invite your child to describe what he or she sees there, using as many adjectives as possible.

- Have your child list three things you can smell, feel, taste, or see in a particular room of the house or on a "senses walk."

- Have your child identify as many parts of the human body as he or she can. Ask him or her to describe the function of each part, if possible.

- Ask your child to read a recipe with you for a simple dish. Practice measuring skills by simulating measuring out the ingredients with water or rice in measuring spoons or cups.

- Have your child read the price of items in a store or supermarket. Challenge him or her to estimate how much can be bought with a designated amount of money. Can your child figure out how much change is left over?

- Encourage your child to tell you whether certain objects in your home (sofa, pencil) would be measured in pounds or ounces.

- Fill a measuring cup with water to different levels, and invite your child to read the measurement and then write it as a fraction.

- Encourage your child to read nonfiction library books and make up creative stories about the subject matter (e.g., lions or airplanes).

6

Assessment

Circle the best answer for each question.

1. What is the middle vowel sound in the picture?

   A. a   **B.** e

   C. i   **D.** u

2. Choose the picture with the same vowel sound as *boat*.

   A.   **B.**

   C.   **D.**

3. Which word has the same sound as the underlined letters in the word h<u>at</u>?

   A. dog   **B.** bird

   C. cat   **D.** fish

4. Choose the word with the same meaning as *finish*.

   A. end   **B.** begin

   C. wish   **D.** find

5. What is the opposite of *clean*?

   A. nice   **B.** dirty

   C. mean   **D.** clear

6. Which of these events happened last?

   A. First, Billy took a bite.   **B.** Then, Billy took a drink of water.

   C. Finally, Billy ate dessert.   **D.** Next, Billy wiped his mouth.

Assessment

7. Write *C* in front of the sentence that tells the cause. Write *E* in front of the sentence that tells the effect.

Maggie left her notebook on the school bus.

Maggie couldn't study for her history test.

8. What word does not belong with the other words?

A.	car	**B.**	truck
C.	school	**D.**	van

Read the passage to answer questions 9–11.

Johnny Appleseed planted apple seeds for 49 years. He lived over 200 years ago. His real name was John Chapman. He walked barefoot around the country planting apple orchards. Some of the apple trees he planted still make apples.

9. Choose the title that tells what the story is about.

A.	Making Apple Pie	**B.**	Walking Barefoot
C.	Johnny Appleseed	**D.**	Eating an Apple

10. What is not a fact about Johnny Appleseed?

A. He planted apple seeds.

B. His real name was John Chapman.

C. He was a nice man.

D. He lived over 200 years ago.

11. Johnny Appleseed planted apple seeds for how many years?

A.	30	**B.**	49
C.	200	**D.**	2

12. The game was over. The team yelled, "Three cheers for Jim!" What probably happened?

A.	Jim went to school.	**B.**	Jim forgot the game.
C.	Jim scored a goal.	**D.**	The team ate dinner.

Assessment

13. Kevin likes to shop with his mom. Kevin pushes the cart. His mom picks food to put in the cart. Where is Kevin?

    A. a toy store   **B.** home

    C. a store that sells food   **D.** school

14. Follow the directions.

    A. Draw a square.

    B. Write *dog* above the square.

    C. Draw a circle inside the square.

Read the story to answer questions 15–17.

Harry and Matt went outside to play baseball. They played in their backyard. Justin and Dan came to play, too. Matt threw the ball to Dan. Dan swung the bat. He missed the ball. Matt threw the ball again. Dan hit the ball hard. It flew over Matt's head. All the boys yelled, "Oh, no!" The ball was heading toward a window.

15. What do you think will happen?

    A. Dan will hit a home run.   **B.** Matt will catch the ball.

    C. Justin will throw the ball.   **D.** The ball will hit a window.

16. Where does this story take place?

    A. a baseball field   **B.** a house

    C. a backyard   **D.** a school

17. What is the main idea of the story?

    A. Dan hit the ball.

    B. Harry and Matt went outside to play baseball.

    C. The ball was heading toward the window.

    D. Justin and Dan came to play, too.

Assessment Analysis

Answer Key:
1. A.
2. C.
3. C.
4. A.
5. B.
6. C.
7. C, E
8. C.
9. C.
10. C.
11. B.
12. C.
13. C.
14. Diagram should be drawn correctly.
15. D.
16. C.
17. B.

After reviewing the assessment, match the problems answered incorrectly to the corresponding activity pages. Your child should spend extra time on those skills to strengthen his or her reading skills.

Number	Skill	Activity Page(s)
1.	long vowels	62–65, 70–73
2.	short vowels	14–17, 22–25, 30–31
3.	consonant digraphs	46–49, 54–57
4.	synonyms	32
5.	antonyms	33
6.	sequencing	40
7.	cause and effect	79
8.	classification	86
9.	choosing titles	38
10.	fact or opinion	87
11.	reading for details	78
12.	inference	81
13.	context clues	39
14.	following directions	89
15.	predicting outcomes	88
16.	setting	80
17.	main idea	41

Assessment

Write the numeral that tells how many.

1. ••••••• •••• five ten

_____ _____ _____ _____

Write the missing number.

2. 4 _____ 6   12 _____ 14   18 _____ 20

Circle the number that is less than the other number in each pair.

3. 13 6   18 9   14 41

Solve each problem.

4. ■ ■ ■ + ○ ○ ○ ○

_____ + _____ = _____

5. ☆ ☆ ✳ ✳ ✳

_____ − _____ = _____

6.

$$\begin{array}{r} 3 \\ +\,2 \\ \hline \end{array} \qquad \begin{array}{r} 0 \\ +\,5 \\ \hline \end{array} \qquad \begin{array}{r} 4 \\ +\,4 \\ \hline \end{array} \qquad \begin{array}{r} 6 \\ +\,2 \\ \hline \end{array} \qquad \begin{array}{r} 5 \\ +\,1 \\ \hline \end{array}$$

7.

$$\begin{array}{r} 7 \\ -\,5 \\ \hline \end{array} \qquad \begin{array}{r} 6 \\ -\,2 \\ \hline \end{array} \qquad \begin{array}{r} 3 \\ -\,1 \\ \hline \end{array} \qquad \begin{array}{r} 5 \\ -\,3 \\ \hline \end{array} \qquad \begin{array}{r} 10 \\ -\,8 \\ \hline \end{array}$$

Write the equations for each fact family.

8. 2, 3, 5

_____ + _____ = _____

_____ + _____ = _____

_____ − _____ = _____

_____ − _____ = _____

9. 4, 7, 11

_____ + _____ = _____

_____ + _____ = _____

_____ − _____ = _____

_____ − _____ = _____

Write the time shown on each clock.

10.

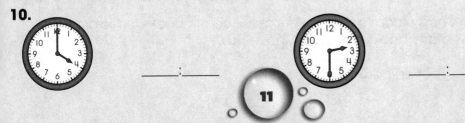

_____ : _____   _____ : _____

Assessment

Count the coin values. Write how much.

11. _____

12. _____

Write the length of each line.

13. _____

14. _____

inches **1** **2**

1 2 3 4 5 6 7

Write how much of each shape is shaded.

15. _____   _____   _____

Draw what comes next.

16. star circle star circle _____

17. star star triangle star star _____

Write the name of each shape.

18.

_____   _____   _____   _____

Solve the problems.

19. Sara went to the store. She bought 4 green apples and 2 red apples. How many apples did Sara buy?

_____ apples

20. Mark had 6 comic books. He gave 2 comic books to his brother. How many books does Mark have now?

_____ comic books

Assessment Analysis

Answer Key:
1. 7, 4, 5, 10
2. 5, 13, 19
3. 6, 9, 14
4. 3 + 4 = 7
5. 5 - 3 = 2
6. 5, 5, 8, 8, 6
7. 2, 4, 2, 2, 2
8. Answers may be in another order.

2 + 3 = 5, 3 + 2 = 5, 5 - 3 = 2, 5 - 2 = 3
9. Answers may be in another order.
4 + 7 = 11, 7 + 4 = 11, 11 - 7 = 4, 11 - 4 = 7
10. 4:00, 2:30
11. 6¢ or $0.06
12. 12¢ or $0.12

13. 2 inches
14. 5 centimeters
15. $\frac{1}{2}, \frac{3}{4}, \frac{2}{3}$
16. ☆
17. ▼
18. triangle, circle, rectangle, square
19. 6 apples
20. 4 comic books

After reviewing the assessment, match the problems answered incorrectly to the corresponding activity pages. Your child should spend extra time on those activities to strengthen his or her math skills.

Number	Skill	Activity Page(s)
1., 2., 3.	numeration	18–21, 26–29, 34–36
4., 6.	addition	37, 43–45, 50
5., 7.	subtraction	51–53, 58–60
8., 9.	fact families	61, 66
10., 11., 12.	time and money	67–69, 74–75
13., 14.	measurement	76–77, 82
15.	fractions	83–84
16., 17., 18.	patterns and geometry	85, 90–91
19., 20.	problem solving	92–93

Sam and Max

Read the poem below.

Sam has a tan cat.

Max is Sam's cat.

Sam has a cap and a hat.

Sam has a bag and a bat.

Sam can tap the bat.

Max ran to the bag and sat.

Max naps and naps on the bag.

Sam and Max

After reading "Sam and Max," answer the following questions.

1. Write four words from the story that rhyme with *mat*.

    _____   _____   _____   _____

2. What is the name of Sam's cat? _____

3. Name four other things listed in this story that Sam has.

    _____   _____   _____   _____

4. Name another word that rhymes with

    bag _____   tap _____   tan _____

5. Why do you think Max ran to the bag? _____
    _____

6. Draw and label a picture of Sam and Max.

Meg the Vet

Read the poem below.

Meg is a vet.

Vets help sick pets.

Vets help pets get well.

Some vets help big pets.

Some vets help little pets.

A vet can wrap a dog's leg.

A vet can mend a horse with a cut.

A vet can fix a cat with no pep.

A vet can help your pet, too.

Meg likes being a vet.

Meg the Vet

After reading "Meg the Vet," answer the following questions.

1. Which sentence tells the main idea?

   A. Pets get hurt a lot.

   B. Vets help pets.

   C. Cats have no pep.

2. Write a *T* for things that are true about vets. Write an *F* for things that are false.

   _____ Vets help pets.

   _____ A vet can help a horse.

   _____ Vets drive buses.

   _____ A vet can wrap a dog's leg.

   _____ Vets sell cars.

   _____ Vets fix bikes.

   _____ Vets mend horses with cuts.

3. How does the story say a vet can help a dog?

   A. mend a cat

   B. wrap a leg

   C. fix a cut

4. What is a vet?

   A. a pet doctor

   B. a people doctor

   C. a truck driver

5. Draw a line from each animal to its group.

	gerbil
Big pets	horse
	hamster
	cow
Little pets	mouse
	sheep

6. List three words with the short *e* sound from the poem.

   _____

   _____

   _____

Introduction to Number Words

Trace the number words.

one

two

three

four

five

six

seven

eight

nine

ten

Quantity

Circle the numeral that tells how many there are of each item.

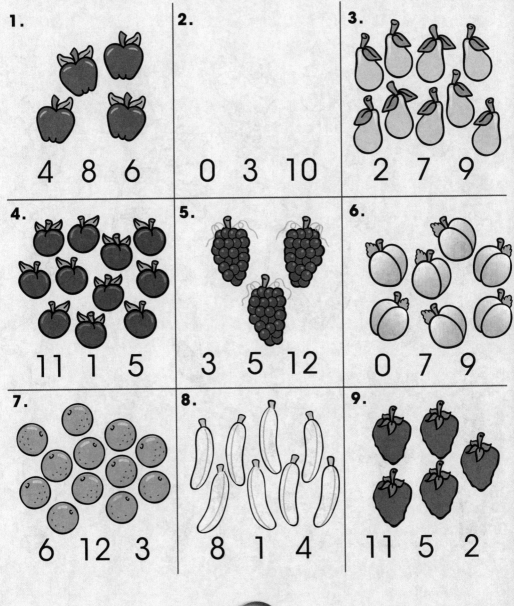

1.

4   8   6

2.

0   3   10

3.

2   7   9

4.

11   1   5

5.

3   5   12

6.

0   7   9

7.

6   12   3

8.

8   1   4

9.

11   5   2

Matching Equal Amounts

Look at the numeral on each bee. Then, draw a line from the bee to the flower with the matching number of petals.

20

Ordinal Numbers

Ordinal numbers tell something's place in line. The mitten is first. The book is second. The strawberry is third.

Study the example above. Then, follow the instructions.

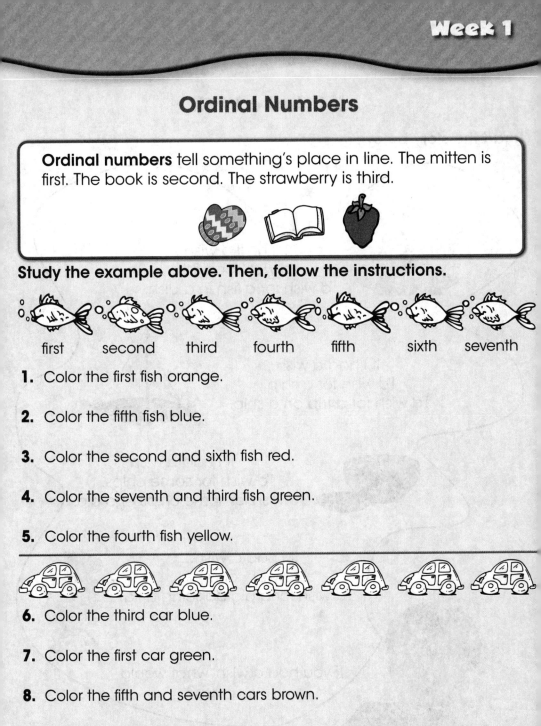

first   second   third   fourth   fifth   sixth   seventh

1. Color the first fish orange.

2. Color the fifth fish blue.

3. Color the second and sixth fish red.

4. Color the seventh and third fish green.

5. Color the fourth fish yellow.

6. Color the third car blue.

7. Color the first car green.

8. Color the fifth and seventh cars brown.

9. Color the second and fourth cars red.

10. Color the sixth car black.

If I Had a Wish

Read the story below.

If I had a wish...
I'd wish for a fish.
I'd wish for a fish in a dish.

If I had a wish...
I'd wish for a ship.
I'd wish for a trip on a ship.

If I had a wish...
I'd wish for some chips.
I'd wish for some chips and dip.

If I had a wish...
I'd wish for a pig.
I'd wish for a pig dancing a jig.

If you had a wish, what would
you wish?

22

If I Had a Wish

After reading "If I Had a Wish," answer the following questions.

1. What could be a new title for this poem?
   A. Wishes
   B. Fish, Ships, and Pigs
   C. A Pig Can Jig

2. Draw a line between the rhyming words that were paired up in the story.

fish	dip
ship	jig
chip	dish
pig	trip

3. What does *jig* mean?
   A. a little dance
   B. a story
   C. a pet

4. Write *Y* if you think the wish could come true. Write *N* if you do not think the wish could come true.

   _____ a fish in a dish

   _____ a ship for a trip

   _____ chips and dip

   _____ a pig dancing a jig

5. What would you wish for?

   _____

   _____

   _____

Pot of Gold

Read the story below.

One day, Josh went outside to play. He saw a big pot.

"Where is the gold?" Josh asked. "Pots always have gold."

Josh looked for the gold. He stomped his foot.

"Who has my gold?" he said.

Suddenly, a little man jumped out.

"You took my gold!" said Josh.

"No," said the little man. "You took my pot."

"This is your pot?" asked Josh.

"Yes," said the little man.

"I'm sorry. Here you go." Josh gave the little man his pot.

The little man gave Josh some gold.

Pot of Gold

After reading "Pot of Gold," answer the following questions.

1. Which sentence tells the main lesson of the story?

   A. If you find something, it belongs to you.

   B. Give things back to the person they belong to.

   C. Pots and gold always go together.

2. Write a *T* by each sentence that is true. Write an *F* by each sentence that is false.

  _____ Josh found a pot.

  _____ The pot belonged to Josh.

  _____ The little man gave Josh some gold.

  _____ Josh lost his gold.

3. Why did Josh stomp his foot?

   A. There was no gold in the pot.

   B. The pot had gold.

   C. The man had no gold.

4. Fill in the missing words from the story.

    pots   man   gold

   A. Josh gave the little _____ the pot.

   B. The little man gave Josh some _____.

   C. Josh thinks that _____ always have gold.

5. Why did the little man give Josh some gold?

   A. for being honest

   B. because he had extra

   C. because Josh asked for some

6. What is the opposite of *little*?

   A. big

   B. small

   C. nice

Skip Counting by Twos

Skip counting is a way to count faster than counting by ones. Skip the same amount of numbers each time.

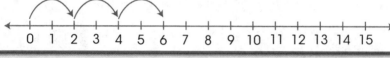

Study the number line above. Then, count by twos. Color each square that you count yellow. The first row has been done for you.

0	1	2	3	4	5	6	7
8	9	10	11	12	13	14	15
16	17	18	19	20	21	22	23
24	25	26	27	28	29	30	31
32	33	34	35	36	37	38	39
40	41	42	43	44	45	46	47
48	49	50	51	52	53	54	55

Write the numerals from the squares that you colored.

  0   2   4   6   ___ ___ ___ ___

  ___ ___ ___ ___ ___ ___ ___ ___

  ___ ___ ___ ___ ___ ___ ___ ___

  ___ ___ ___ ___ ___

Counting by Fives

One way to count to 100 is to count by **fives.** Practice counting by fives using the number line.

5 10 15 20 25 30 35 40 45 50 55 60 65 70 75 80 85 90 95 100

Study the number line above. Then, count by fives to 100. Write the numerals on the hands. Use the fingers to help you count.

Counting by Tens

Another way to count to 100 is by using **tens.** Practice counting to 100 by tens using the number line.

Study the number line above. Then, count by tens to connect each group of dots. For each picture, start at 0.

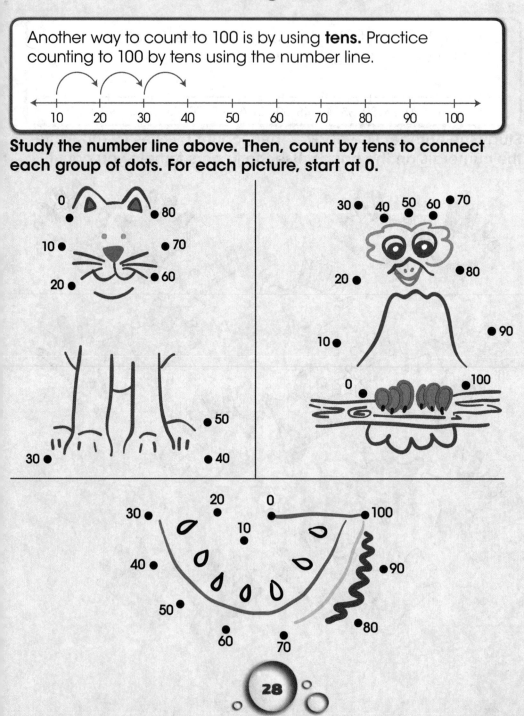

Numbers In Between

0	1	2	3	4	5	6	7	8	9	10	11	12	13	14	15	16	17	18	19	20

Count the sets of objects in each box. Then, write the numeral that is in between the two amounts. Use the number line above to help you.

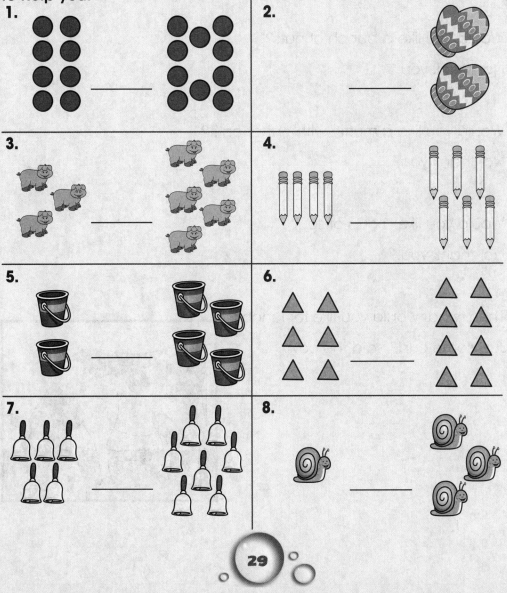

"What's For Lunch?"

Read the story below.

"Would you like a hot dog on a bun?"

"No, thank you."

"Would you like a bunch of nuts?"

"No, thank you."

"Would you like a muffin with butter on it?"

"No, thank you."

"Would you like a cup of soup?"

"No, thank you."

"Then, what would you like for lunch?"

"Just some cud," said the cow.

"What's For Lunch?"

After reading "What's for Lunch?," answer the following questions.

1. In the story, who is being asked, "What would you like for lunch?"

    A. a boy

    B. a cow

    C. a mother

2. Number what the cow was offered for lunch in order.

    _____ soup

    _____ nuts

    _____ hot dog on a bun

    _____ muffin

3. What did the cow want to eat for lunch?

    A. a hot dog on a bun

    B. some cud

    C. a muffin with butter

4. Number the foods in the order that you would like to eat them. Start with your first choice.

    _____ hot dog

    _____ nuts

    _____ muffin

    _____ soup

5. What does *cud* mean?

    A. a dessert

    B. something cows chew

    C. something to drink

Super Synonyms

Synonyms are words that have the same meaning.
Examples: small, little   big, huge

Read the word on each snowman. Choose a word in the word box
that has the same meaning. Then, write the word under the snowman.

choose	sleep	run
keep	quick	kind

1. fast

    _____

2. save

    _____

3. nice

    _____

4. rest

    _____

5. jog

    _____

6. pick

    _____

Awesome Antonyms

Antonyms are words that have opposite meanings.
Examples: fast, slow   good, bad

Draw a line from each word on the right to the word on the left with the opposite meaning.

1. day   little

2. long   night

3. big   new

4. hot   short

5. old   under

6. over   cold

Less Than

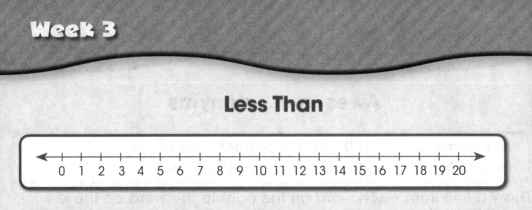

Study the number line above. Then, circle the group in each box that has less objects.

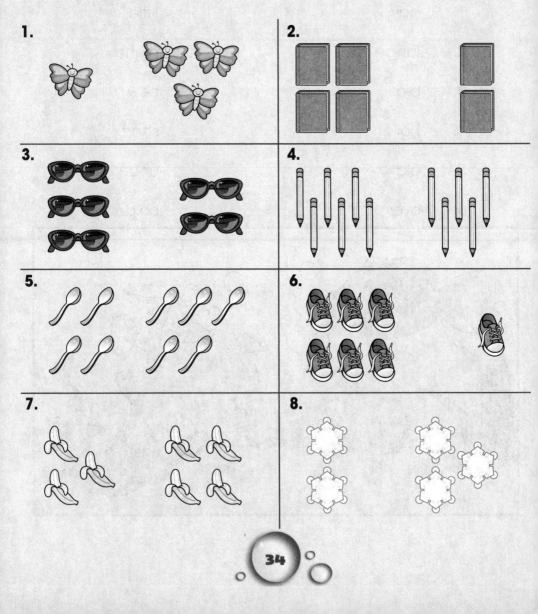

More Than

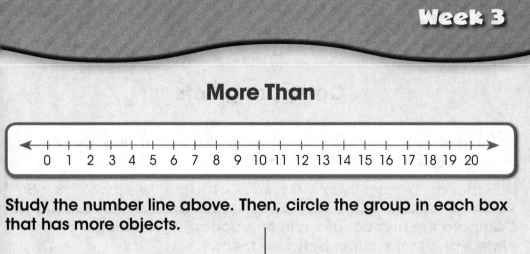

Study the number line above. Then, circle the group in each box that has more objects.

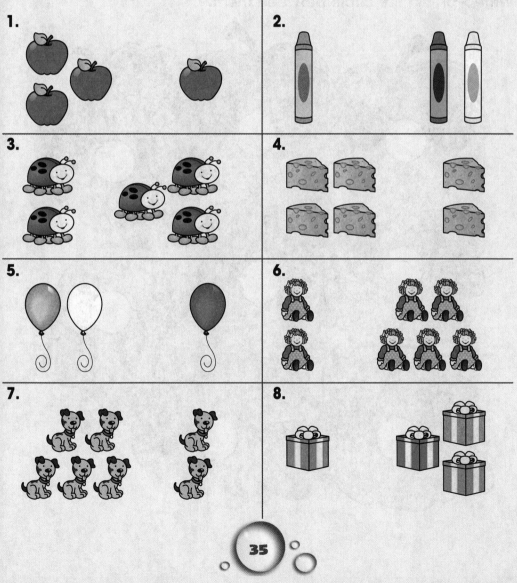

1.

2.

3.

4.

5.

6.

7.

8.

Comparing Sets

There is a short way to write **"greater than"** and **"less than"** using signs. Their signs look like this:

> means "greater than"   **9 > 5**   < means "less than"   **3 < 8**

Compare the number of spots on each set of ladybugs.
Write > or < in the circle between them.

Adding 0-6

Two carrots and 3 carrots makes 5 carrots altogether.
The mathematical way to say this is "2 **plus** 3 **equals** 5."
Five is the **sum.**

Color 2 carrots green.
Color 3 carrots orange.
How many carrots are there altogether?

$$\begin{array}{r} 2 \\ + 3 \\ \hline \boxed{5} \end{array}$$

Study the example above. Then, color the pictures below. Count the objects. Write the sum in each box.

1. Color 1 button blue.
   Color 3 buttons red.
   How many buttons are there altogether?

$$\begin{array}{r} 1 \\ + 3 \\ \hline \boxed{4} \end{array}$$

2. Color 4 apples red.
   Color 2 apples yellow.
   How many apples are there altogether?

$$\begin{array}{r} 4 \\ + 2 \\ \hline \boxed{6} \end{array}$$

3. Color 2 stars yellow.
   Color 2 stars blue.
   How many stars are there altogether?

$$\begin{array}{r} 2 \\ + 2 \\ \hline \boxed{4} \end{array}$$

4. Color 1 ball red.
   Color 4 balls yellow.
   How many balls are there altogether?

$$\begin{array}{r} 1 \\ + 4 \\ \hline \boxed{5} \end{array}$$

It's Time for Titles

The title of a picture or a story tells what it is about. Circle the best title for each picture.

1.

Fish in the Sea

My Pet Fish

2.

A Trip to the Moon

Planet Earth

3.

A Day at the Beach

Fun at the Pool

4.

A Bird Adventure

The Plane Ride

5.

I'm All Wet!

The Rainbow

6.

The Cat and Dog

The Cat Picture

Write your own title for the picture.

7.

a DOg is DrinKing

Clues for You

Read each clue. Find the word in the list that makes sense in the blank. Then, write the word from the list in the puzzle.

1. m a k
2. h e l i v e
3. l i v e
4. k i n d
5. u n d e r
   e
   p

Across

3. Bees _____ in hives.

4. A dog is one _____ of pet.

5. Ants live _____ the ground.

Down

1. Some birds _____ nests.

2. You can _____ your friend's hand.

4. Birds sit on eggs to _____ them warm.

Word List

~~keep~~
~~kind~~
~~live~~
~~hold~~
~~make~~
~~under~~

All Mixed Up

Sequencing means putting events from a story in the order they happened. A picture story can be put in order by looking at details in the pictures.

Number the pictures in the order they would happen.

Wheels

Read each passage. Read the choices. Circle the main idea for each passage.

1.   Wheels help us do work. They make it easy to move things. If cars, trucks, and trains didn't have wheels, they would not go. If a bike did not have wheels, it would not roll.

Trains have wheels.

Bikes can roll.

Wheels make things easy to move.

2.   A long time ago, men and women carried things on their backs. Donkeys and camels carried things in packs. Sometimes, they dragged things behind them. It was hard to move things without wheels. Men and women could not go far. Donkeys and camels could not carry very much.

Donkeys carry things in packs.

People had to move things without wheels.

People had to carry things on their backs.

41

Writing Addition Equations

Here are 2 groups of dogs. One group has 4 dogs. One group has 3 dogs. There are 7 dogs altogether. The mathematical way to write this is **4 + 3 = 7.** This is called an **addition equation.**

Study the example above. Then, write an equation for each picture.

1.

$$4 + 1 = 5$$

2.

$$3 + 2 = 5$$

3.

$$3 + 3 = 6$$

4.

$$4 + 2 = 6$$

5.

$$1 + 2 = 3$$

6.

$$1 + 3 = 4$$

Addition Practice

Study the examples on page 42. Then, solve each problem.

$$\begin{array}{r} 1 \\ + 6 \\ \hline 7 \end{array}$$

$$\begin{array}{r} 3 \\ + 4 \\ \hline 7 \end{array}$$

$$\begin{array}{r} 2 \\ + 6 \\ \hline 8 \end{array}$$

$$\begin{array}{r} 3 \\ + 5 \\ \hline 8 \end{array}$$

$$\begin{array}{r} 2 \\ + 1 \\ \hline 3 \end{array}$$

$$\begin{array}{r} 8 \\ + 1 \\ \hline 9 \end{array}$$

$$\begin{array}{r} 6 \\ + 2 \\ \hline 8 \end{array}$$

$$\begin{array}{r} 4 \\ + 5 \\ \hline 9 \end{array}$$

$$\begin{array}{r} 2 \\ + 4 \\ \hline 6 \end{array}$$

$$\begin{array}{r} 1 \\ + 7 \\ \hline 8 \end{array}$$

$$\begin{array}{r} 1 \\ + 3 \\ \hline 4 \end{array}$$

$$\begin{array}{r} 3 \\ + 2 \\ \hline 5 \end{array}$$

$$\begin{array}{r} 2 \\ + 7 \\ \hline 9 \end{array}$$

$$\begin{array}{r} 5 \\ + 2 \\ \hline 7 \end{array}$$

$$\begin{array}{r} 4 \\ + 3 \\ \hline 1 \end{array}$$

$$\begin{array}{r} 3 \\ + 6 \\ \hline 9 \end{array}$$

$$\begin{array}{r} 4 \\ + 1 \\ \hline 5 \end{array}$$

$$\begin{array}{r} 5 \\ + 1 \\ \hline 6 \end{array}$$

Coloring Doubles

Solve each problem. Then, color all of the spaces in which you are adding doubles orange. Color the other spaces blue.

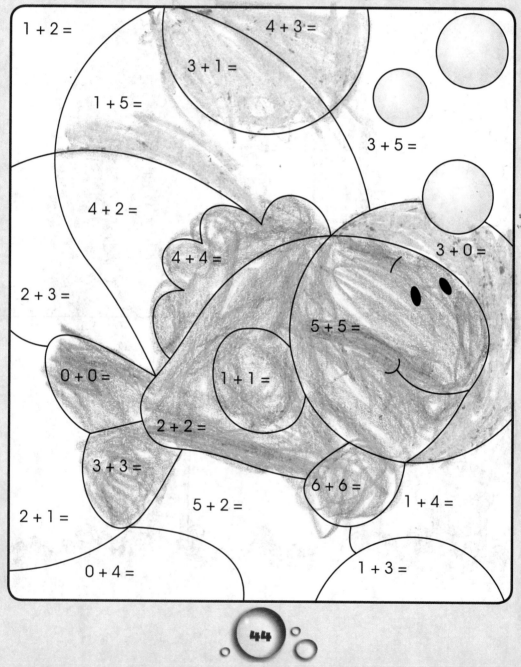

1 + 2 =

4 + 3 =

3 + 1 =

1 + 5 =

3 + 5 =

4 + 2 =

4 + 4 =

3 + 0 =

2 + 3 =

5 + 5 =

0 + 0 =

1 + 1 =

2 + 2 =

3 + 3 =

6 + 6 =

1 + 4 =

2 + 1 =

5 + 2 =

0 + 4 =

1 + 3 =

Column Addition

Add the first 2 numbers. 2 + 7 = 9.
Then, add the last number. 9 + 4 = 13.

$$\begin{array}{r} 2 \\ 7 \\ +\ 4 \\ \end{array} \quad \begin{array}{r} 9 \\ +\ 4 \\ \hline 13 \end{array}$$

Study the example above. Then, solve each problem.

1.

$$\begin{array}{r} 3 \\ 3 \\ +\ 8 \\ \hline \end{array} \qquad \begin{array}{r} 4 \\ 5 \\ +\ 2 \\ \hline \end{array} \qquad \begin{array}{r} 7 \\ 2 \\ +\ 1 \\ \hline \end{array} \qquad \begin{array}{r} 2 \\ 3 \\ +\ 7 \\ \hline \end{array} \qquad \begin{array}{r} 5 \\ 3 \\ +\ 7 \\ \hline \end{array}$$

2.

$$\begin{array}{r} 7 \\ 2 \\ +\ 6 \\ \hline \end{array} \qquad \begin{array}{r} 8 \\ 4 \\ +\ 5 \\ \hline \end{array} \qquad \begin{array}{r} 9 \\ 1 \\ +\ 4 \\ \hline \end{array} \qquad \begin{array}{r} 8 \\ 7 \\ +\ 2 \\ \hline \end{array} \qquad \begin{array}{r} 6 \\ 5 \\ +\ 3 \\ \hline \end{array}$$

3.

$$\begin{array}{r} 5 \\ 7 \\ +\ 3 \\ \hline \end{array} \qquad \begin{array}{r} 4 \\ 7 \\ +\ 2 \\ \hline \end{array} \qquad \begin{array}{r} 8 \\ 5 \\ +\ 1 \\ \hline \end{array} \qquad \begin{array}{r} 3 \\ 4 \\ +\ 3 \\ \hline \end{array} \qquad \begin{array}{r} 6 \\ 2 \\ +\ 5 \\ \hline \end{array}$$

Shh!

Read the poem below.

Shh! The baby's sleeping.
Please shut the door.

Shh! Your sister's napping.
Please don't shout.

Shh! Your dad is snoozing.
Please don't turn on the television.

Shh! Your grandpa's snoring.
Please don't shake your tambourine.

Shh! It's your bedtime.
Hush and shut your eyes.

Shh!

After reading "Shh!," answer the following questions.

1. Which sentence tells the main idea?
   - **A.** Children are too loud.
   - **B.** Moms like it quiet.
   - **C.** Be quiet when people are sleeping.

2. Who is "Shh!" probably being said to?
   - **A.** mom
   - **B.** child
   - **C.** dad

3. Who is probably saying "Shh!"?
   - **A.** Mom
   - **B.** Dad
   - **C.** teacher

4. Circle the people who are sleeping.

   Mom   baby

   sister   Dad

   Grandma   Grandpa

5. What do you like to do to make noise?

   _____

   _____

   _____

   _____

   _____

6. Write an X by the words that mean the same as *sleeping*.

   _____ napping

   _____ snoozing

   _____ shouting

   _____ laughing

47

Uncle Rich

Read the poem below.

Our Uncle Rich always says,
"Children, choose one thing.
Anything you ask for,
that's the thing I'll bring."

Chad chose a choo choo train.
Chip chose a chair.
Chan chose a chopper toy
that flies in the air.

Chet chose some chocolate.
Chuck chose a chestnut.
Chester chose checkers,
his favorite game.

Uncle Rich brought each child
that one favorite thing.
But more than things,
it's joy that our favorite uncle brings.

Uncle Rich

After reading "Uncle Rich," answer the following questions.

1. Which sentence tells the main idea of the poem?
- **A.** Children like toys.
- **B.** Uncle Rich brings gifts.
- **C.** Uncle Rich has lots of money.

2. What does Uncle Rich bring that is better than things?
- **A.** anything
- **B.** chopper
- **C.** joy

3. What do the children get to choose?
- **A.** a chair
- **B.** one thing
- **C.** game

4. What does *joy* mean?
- **A.** money
- **B.** presents
- **C.** happiness

5. Group the following things.

choo choo train   chair

chopper toy   chocolate

chestnut   checkers

Toy	Not a Toy

6. Draw a line between each pair of rhyming words.

thing   rain

chain   chair

air   bring

Finding the Sum of 3 Addends

Study the example on page 45. Then, solve each problem.

Math is fun!

1. 6 + 4 + 2 =

5 + 4 + 6 =

4 + 3 + 7 =

6 + 2 + 8 =

9 + 4 + 3 =

5 + 4 + 9 =

7 + 2 + 5 =

6 + 2 + 6 =

2. 3 + 2 + 4 =

1 + 1 + 1 =

7 + 3 + 2 =

4 + 4 + 8 =

2 + 2 + 4 =

3 + 4 + 3 =

2 + 8 + 7 =

3 + 3 + 7 =

4 + 3 + 8 =

3 + 3 + 3 =

50

Subtracting 0–7

Three bunches of grapes take away 2 bunches of grapes leaves 1 bunch of grapes. The mathematical way to say this is "3 **minus** 2 **equals** 1." One is the **difference**.

$$\begin{array}{r} 3 \\ -\ 2 \\ \hline \boxed{1} \end{array}$$

Study the example above. Then, cross out the objects to be subtracted. Solve each problem.

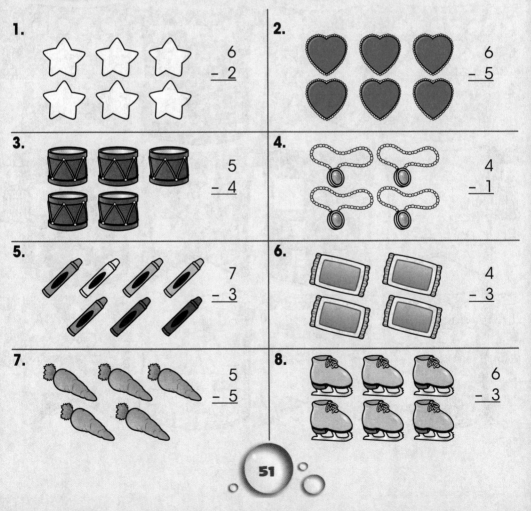

1.
$$\begin{array}{r} 6 \\ -\ 2 \\ \hline \end{array}$$

2.
$$\begin{array}{r} 6 \\ -\ 5 \\ \hline \end{array}$$

3.
$$\begin{array}{r} 5 \\ -\ 4 \\ \hline \end{array}$$

4.
$$\begin{array}{r} 4 \\ -\ 1 \\ \hline \end{array}$$

5.
$$\begin{array}{r} 7 \\ -\ 3 \\ \hline \end{array}$$

6.
$$\begin{array}{r} 4 \\ -\ 3 \\ \hline \end{array}$$

7.
$$\begin{array}{r} 5 \\ -\ 5 \\ \hline \end{array}$$

8.
$$\begin{array}{r} 6 \\ -\ 3 \\ \hline \end{array}$$

Subtracting from 10 and Less

Study the example on page 51. Then, use the pictures to help you solve each problem.

1. 8 − 3 =

7 − 2 =

10 − 4 =

9 − 3 =

2. 10 − 5 =

8 − 4 =

5 − 2 =

7 − 3 =

3. 6 − 3 =

4 − 2 =

9 − 5 =

10 − 6 =

4. 8 − 5 =

6 − 4 =

9 − 4 =

10 − 4 =

Differences of 2 or 3

Solve each problem. Then, color the spaces with a difference of 2 or 3 yellow. Color the other spaces purple.

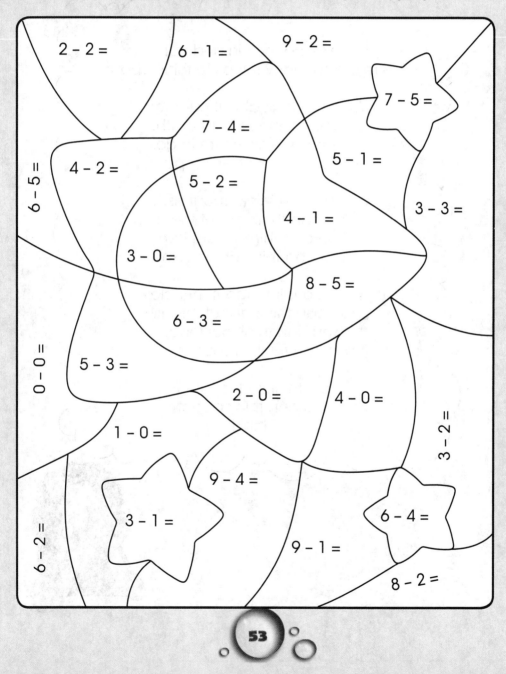

2 − 2 =

6 − 1 =

9 − 2 =

7 − 5 =

7 − 4 =

6 − 5 =

4 − 2 =

5 − 2 =

5 − 1 =

3 − 3 =

4 − 1 =

3 − 0 =

8 − 5 =

6 − 3 =

0 − 0 =

5 − 3 =

2 − 0 =

4 − 0 =

1 − 0 =

3 − 2 =

9 − 4 =

3 − 1 =

6 − 4 =

9 − 1 =

6 − 2 =

8 − 2 =

This and That

Read the poem below.

This and that, in and out.
There are so many things to think about.

You can think about numbers.
You can think about math.
You can think where to go.
You can think of which path.

You can think about us.
You can think about them.
You can think about her.
You can think about him.

You can think about thimbles.
You can think about thread.
You can think out loud.
You can think in your head.

Just think of the things
you can think about.
Think!

This and That

After reading "This and That," answer the following questions.

1. Circle another title for this poem.

    A. Things to Think About

    B. Choosing the Right Path

    C. Thimbles and Thread

2. Name four things the poem says you can think about.

_____

_____

_____

_____

3. What else can you think about? Think!

_____

_____

_____

_____

_____

_____

4. Draw a line between each pair of rhyming words.

    math   about

    out   head

    thread   path

5. Write the words in the correct groups below.

    this   math

    that   think

    there   things

_th_ sound in _thin_	_th_ sound in _then_
_____	_____
_____	_____
_____	_____

55

Questions

Read the poem below.

What should we do?
Watch a whale whack the wharf?
Whine about a wheel that's broken?
Whirl in circles on a whim?

Where should we go?
Where the wheat whips in the wind?
Where you can whistle while you work?
Where a whale whiffs the breeze?

When should we go?
When the man with white whiskers whispers, "Now"?
When the wind whistles which way to go?
When the wheel of the wagon has been fixed?

Questions

After reading "Questions," answer the following questions.

1. This is a nonsense poem. What does *nonsense* mean?

    A. does not rhyme

    B. does not make sense

    C. asks good questions

2. Number these activities in the order that you would most like to do them.

    _____ watch a whale

    _____ whine about a wheel

    _____ whirl in circles

3. Where would you go to see a whale whiff the breeze?

    A. the ocean

    B. the farm

    C. the zoo

4. What would you like to do?

_____

_____

_____

_____

_____

_____

5. Circle all of the *wh* words in the poem. Write four of the *wh* words.

_____

_____

_____

_____

Subtraction Scramble

Solve the problems. Unscramble the letters in boxes with the same differences to spell 5 animal names. Use the words in the box to help you. Write the names of the animals on the lines.

3 – 1 = _____ C	2 – 2 = _____ C	7 – 3 = _____ A
6 – 5 = _____ M	5 – 3 = _____ W	3 – 2 = _____ S
3 – 3 = _____ D	6 – 4 = _____ O	4 – 1 = _____ D
5 – 4 = _____ O	7 – 4 = _____ O	4 – 4 = _____ K
6 – 3 = _____ G	5 – 5 = _____ U	6 – 2 = _____ C
2 – 1 = _____ U	5 – 1 = _____ T	4 – 3 = _____ E

CAT	COW	MOUSE	DUCK	DOG

DIFFERENCE	LETTERS	ANIMAL
0	__ __ __ __	_____
1	__ __ __ __ __	_____
2	__ __ __	_____
3	__ __ __	_____
4	__ __ __	_____

Writing Subtraction Equations

Here is a group of 7 dogs. Four dogs go home. Three dogs stay. The mathematical way to write this is **7 – 4 = 3**. This is called a **subtraction equation**.

Study the example above. Then, write an equation for each picture.

1.

_____ - _____ = _____   _____ - _____ = _____   _____ - _____ = _____

2.

_____ - _____ = _____   _____ - _____ = _____   _____ - _____ = _____

3.

_____ - _____ = _____   _____ - _____ = _____   _____ - _____ = _____

Subtracting from 18 and Less

```
←―――――――――――――――――――――――→
0  1  2  3  4  5  6  7  8  9  10 11 12 13 14 15 16 17 18 19 20
```

Solve each problem. Use the number line to help you.

1.
$$15 - 8$$ $$16 - 7$$ $$18 - 9$$ $$14 - 9$$ $$17 - 9$$

2.
$$17 - 8$$ $$13 - 6$$ $$15 - 6$$ $$16 - 8$$ $$12 - 7$$

3.
$$16 - 9$$ $$14 - 8$$ $$12 - 6$$ $$15 - 7$$ $$12 - 5$$

4.
$$15 - 9$$ $$11 - 4$$ $$17 - 7$$ $$16 - 2$$ $$18 - 4$$

Fact Families

A **fact family** is made up of 3 numbers that are related. The numbers can be used in a set of math problems.

$$\underline{1} + \underline{3} = \underline{4}$$
$$\underline{3} + \underline{1} = \underline{4}$$
$$\underline{4} - \underline{3} = \underline{1}$$
$$\underline{4} - \underline{1} = \underline{3}$$

Study the example above. Then, write 2 addition and 2 subtraction equations for each fact family.

1.

5
3 2

_____ + _____ = _____

_____ + _____ = _____

_____ - _____ = _____

_____ - _____ = _____

2.

4
2 6

_____ + _____ = _____

_____ + _____ = _____

_____ - _____ = _____

_____ - _____ = _____

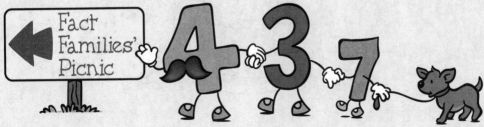

Fact Families' Picnic

The Birthday

Read the story below.

It was Theresa's birthday. She invited Jay, Doris, Gayle, Jane, and Jake. Her friends came at the same time. They were ready for a day of play. They played a game of ball. They went for a hike on a trail. They raced back to eat cake. Theresa opened her gifts. Jay gave her a book. Doris gave her a fake snake. Gayle's gift was a toy monkey with a long tail. Jane gave her a DVD. Jake gave her a doll with a dress. Theresa had a fun birthday.

The Birthday

After reading "The Birthday," answer the following questions.

1. What is the main idea of the story?

    A. going for a hike
    B. Theresa's birthday party
    C. Theresa opening her gifts

2. Put the events from the story in order.

    _____ Jane gave Theresa a DVD.

    _____ They played a game of ball.

    _____ They raced back to eat cake.

    _____ Theresa opened her gifts.

3. What did Doris give Theresa?

    A. a fake snake
    B. a boat with a sail
    C. a monkey with a long tail

4. What presents would you like for your birthday?

_____

_____

_____

_____

_____

5. Write each of the following long *a* words in the correct column.

cake   Gayle   train

sail   play   race

snake   day   Jay

same   tail   trail

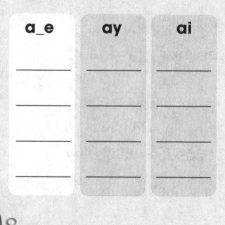

a_e	ay	ai
____	____	____
____	____	____
____	____	____
____	____	____

It's Time

Read the poem below.

It's time for what?
It's time for time!
Whatever is time for?

It's time to go to bed.
It's time to get up.
It's time to eat.

It's time to be good.
It's time to do your best.
It's time to learn.

It's time to go out.
It's time to come in.
It's time to be there.

It's time to grow up.
It's time to stay young.
Whatever your age, it's time.

It's your time to be.
It's my time for me.
Let's be friends, it's time.

It's Time

After reading "It's Time," answer the following questions.

1. Write three words that rhyme with *time*.

_____

_____

_____

2. The poem says, "It's time to eat." What time do you eat these meals?

breakfast _____

lunch _____

dinner _____

3. Write the antonym (opposite) of each of the following words. The words are in the poem if you need help.

in _____

stay_____

here _____

worst _____

old _____

you _____

down _____

stop _____

bad _____

More Fact Families

Study the example on page 61. Then, write 2 addition and 2 subtraction equations for each fact family.

1.

7   5   12

____ + ____ = ____

____ + ____ = ____

____ − ____ = ____

____ − ____ = ____

2.

____ + ____ = ____

____ + ____ = ____

____ − ____ = ____

____ − ____ = ____

8
7
15

3.

____ + ____ = ____

____ + ____ = ____

____ − ____ = ____

____ − ____ = ____

9
8
17

4.

8   6   14

____ + ____ = ____

____ + ____ = ____

____ − ____ = ____

____ − ____ = ____

Telling Time to the Hour

The short hand is called the **hour hand.** It tells the hour. The long hand is the **minute hand.** It tells the minute. This clock's hour hand is on the 8. The minute hand is on the 12. The clock shows 8 o'clock.

8:00

Study the example above. Then, write the time shown on each clock.

1.

_____ o'clock

2.

_____ o'clock

3.

_____ o'clock

4.

_____ o'clock

Telling Time in Half-Hour Increments

When the clock's minute hand is on the 6, the time is 30 minutes after the hour. This clock's hour hand is on the 8. The minute hand is on the 6. The clock shows 8:30.

8:30

Study the examples above and on page 67. Then, write the time shown on each clock.

1.

_____:_____ _____:_____ _____:_____

2.

_____:_____ _____:_____ _____:_____

3.

_____:_____ _____:_____ _____:_____

Elapsed Time

Use the hour hand to tell how long something lasts.

The rain started.
3:00

The rain ended.
5:00

How long did it rain?
2 hours

Study the example above. Then, find how much time has passed in each word problem.

1.
The sun came out from behind the clouds at 1:00. The sun set at 6:00. How long was it out?

_____ hours

2. It began to rain at 2:00. It stopped raining at 4:00. How long did it rain?

_____ hours

3.
The wind started at 12:00. It stopped at 3:00. How long did the wind blow?

_____ hours

4.
The rainbow appeared at 6:00. It disappeared at 8:00. How long was it out?

_____ hours

5. The clouds covered the sky from 5:00 until 8:00. How long did the clouds cover the sky?

_____ hours

Mole

Read the story below.

Mole was not bold. He was shy. He liked to hide in his hole by the road. Toad hopped by Mole's home. He saw a moat all around Mole's home. Toad poked at the moat. It was wet and cold. Toad called, "Hello, Mole! Do I see a moat?"

Mole froze in his hole. He had a boat to sail in his moat. He did not want old Toad to know. A wet toad would soak his boat. Again Toad shouted, "Hello! Do I see a boat for your moat?" Shy Mole wrote a note. He took a long pole. He poked the note up the hole. Toad read the note. It said, "Go away!" It was no joke. Toad sadly hopped down the road.

Next, Goat loped down the road. He saw Mole's home. He saw the moat. He did not care about the moat or the boat. He wanted to eat. He yelled down the hole, "I want to eat! Do you have some roast beef on toast?" This time, Mole was more bold. He told that old goat, "All right, have half a loaf, but don't choke!"

Goat told Mole, "You are a very good host!"

After lunch, Mole went for a float on his boat in the moat.

Mole

After reading "Mole," answer the following questions.

1. What is the main idea of the story?

    A. Mole was not bold. He was shy.

    B. Toad was not bold. He was shy.

    C. Goat was not bold. He was shy.

2. Why didn't Mole want Toad to know about his boat?

    A. Toad would hide in the boat.

    B. Toad would soak his boat.

    C. Toad would mope in the boat.

3. What did Goat want from Mole?

    A. roast beef on toast

    B. gold

    C. to play

4. What is another word for *poked*?

    A. stopped

    B. floated

    C. jabbed

5. What is the meaning of the word *host* in this story?

    A. someone who takes care of a guest

    B. a place for another animal to live

    C. a large number

6. Write the long *o* words in the right group.

hope   boat   froze

note   road   moat

roast   choke

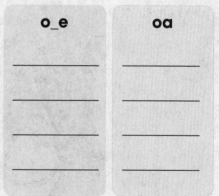

o_e	oa
_____	_____
_____	_____
_____	_____
_____	

Duke and Mule

Read the poem below.

Duke was a dude who lived in the city.

He visited a ranch.

He tried to ride a mule.

The mule was rude.

It did not move.

Duke was not happy.

He sang a tune.

The mule did not like it.

Duke fed the mule.

He gave it a sugar cube.

The mule was happy.

It gave Duke a ride.

Duke and Mule

After reading "Duke and Mule," answer the following questions.

1. What did Duke want to do?

  A. sing a song
  B. rope a horse
  C. ride a mule
  D. feed a cow

2. What did the mule not like?

  A. Duke's song
  B. sugar
  C. hay
  D. work

3. Why did the mule give Duke a ride?

  A. Duke gave the mule a carrot.
  B. Duke gave the mule a sugar cube.
  C. Duke gave the mule an apple.
  D. Duke gave the mule water.

4. What did the mule do when Duke tried to ride him?

  A. It trotted away.
  B. It lay down.
  C. It ran away.
  D. It did not move.

5. Who was Duke?

  A. a dancer
  B. a farmer
  C. a dude who lived in the city

6. Write the six u_e words from the story.

  _____

  _____

  _____

  _____

  _____

  _____

Introduction to Money

Follow these steps to count coins:
1. Count the dimes.
2. Count the nickels.
3. Count the pennies.

10¢ 10¢

5¢ 5¢ 1¢ 1¢

+ + = 16¢

Study the example above. Then, count the coins. Write how much money is in each piggy bank.

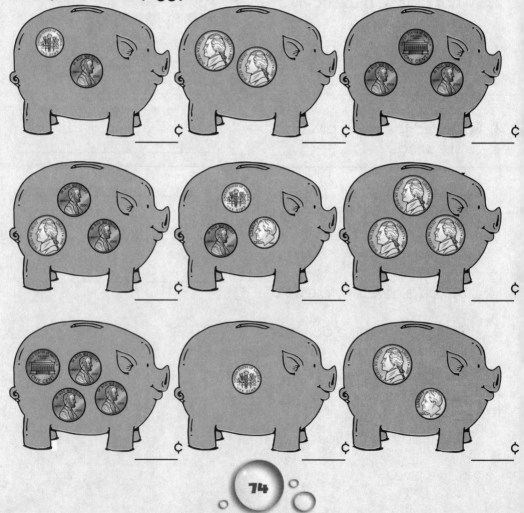

Grouping Coins

There can be many ways to group coins to make the same amount of money. Each group here makes 20¢.

Study the example above. Then, circle a group of coins that equals the amount of money shown in each box.

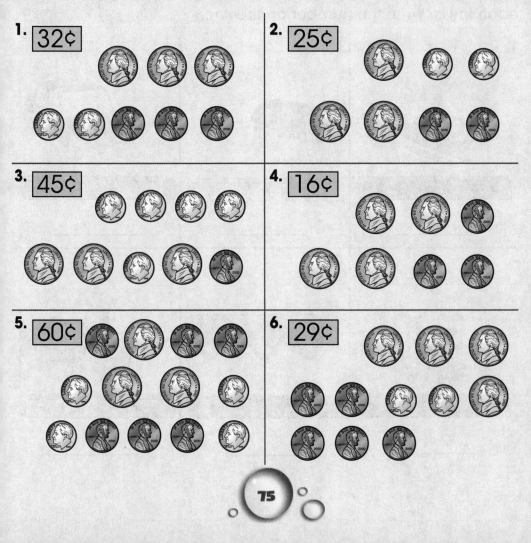

1. 32¢

2. 25¢

3. 45¢

4. 16¢

5. 60¢

6. 29¢

Measuring with Blocks

The boat is 4 cubes long.

Study the example above. Then, count how many cubes long each toy is. Write the number on the line.

Measuring with Inches

This is a **standard** ruler. It measures **inches.** It tells how long an object is.

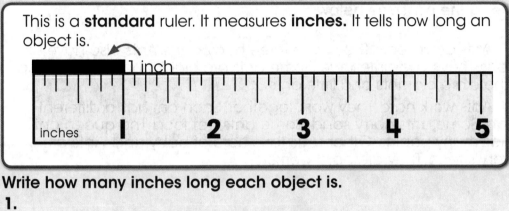

1 inch

inches 1 2 3 4 5

Write how many inches long each object is.

1.

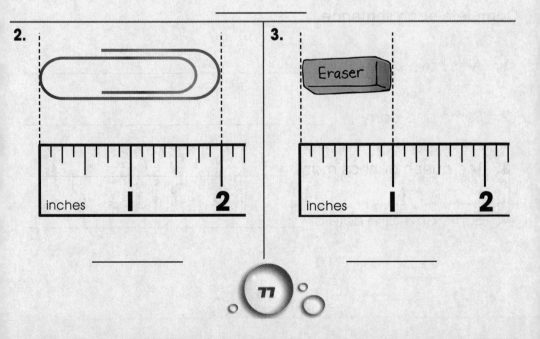

inches 1 2 3 4 5

_____

2.

inches 1 2

_____

3.

Eraser

inches 1 2

_____

Ants

Read the passage below.

Ants are insects. They have three body parts. Ants also have six legs. They have antennae. Some ants are black and some are red. There are big ants and little ants.

Ants work hard. They work together. Each ant has a different job. Some ants carry sand. Some ants get food. The queen ant has many babies. Other ants take care of baby ants. Ants are very strong. They are hard workers.

Draw an ant. Use the details from the passage above.

Complete each sentence.

1. Ants have different _____.

2. Some ants carry _____.

3. The queen ant has many _____.

4. Some ants take care of _____.

It's Cold Outside

A **cause** is what makes something happen.
An **effect** is the thing that happens.

Read each pair of sentences. Write *C* in front of the sentence that tells about the cause. Write *E* in front of the sentence that tells about the effect.

1. _____ It was cold outside.

_____ Tom started shivering.

2. _____ That made his hands warm.

_____ He rubbed his hands together.

3. _____ That made his hands much warmer.

_____ Tom put his mittens on.

79

"Setting" the Stage

The **setting** tells where and when a story takes place. To find what a story's setting is, read the sentences carefully and look for clues.

Read each passage. Then, answer each question.

Tony plays by a body of water. There are ducks swimming in the water. Many trees grow near the water.

1. Where is Tony playing?

    A. near a pond   **B.** by the ocean

    C. at a school   **D.** in his house

There is a busy street near Carly's house. Many cars drive on the street. There is a bus stop in front of her house.

2. Where does Carly live?

    A. at the beach   **B.** in the country

    C. by a river   **D.** in the city

Kristen's family has many animals. A fence is in front of her house. A barn is next to her house.

3. Where does Kristen live?

    A. next to a church   **B.** a farm

    C. in a log cabin   **D.** in an apartment

Story Clues

Read each passage. Then, circle the best answer to the question.

Sue Lee rode to the store. She rode up a big hill. She had to pedal hard. It was easy to ride down the other side. Sue Lee went very fast. She had to use her brakes.

1. What did Sue Lee ride?

a horse   a skateboard   a bike

Sam likes to swing the bat and hit the ball. He loves to run to first base. Sometimes, he even makes it to third base. He wants to play shortstop when he grows up.

2. What game does Sam like?

football   baseball   golf

Measuring with Centimeters

Metric rulers measure in **centimeters**.

1 centimeter

1 2 3 4 5 6 7 8 9 10 11 12

Write how many centimeters long each object is.

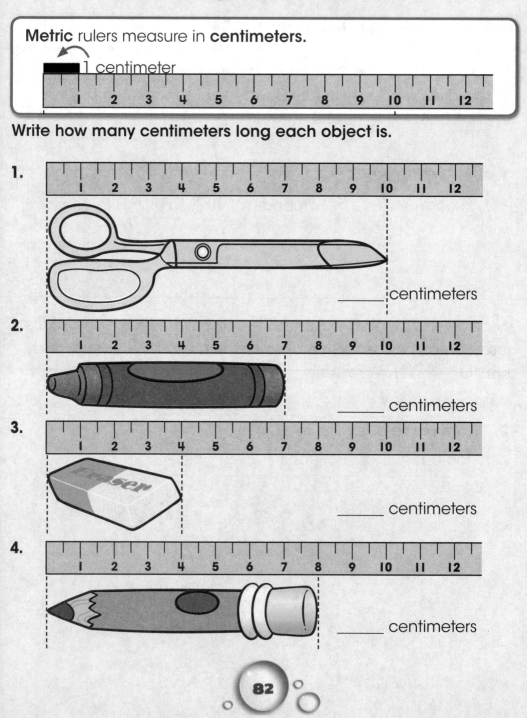

1.

1 2 3 4 5 6 7 8 9 10 11 12

_____ centimeters

2.

1 2 3 4 5 6 7 8 9 10 11 12

_____ centimeters

3.

1 2 3 4 5 6 7 8 9 10 11 12

_____ centimeters

4.

1 2 3 4 5 6 7 8 9 10 11 12

_____ centimeters

Introduction to Fractions

This cracker is cut into 2 equal **parts.** Each part is called **one-half.** We write one-half like this: $\frac{1}{2}$.

The parts of this cracker are not equal. This does not show the fraction $\frac{1}{2}$.

Circle the foods with parts that each show $\frac{1}{2}$.

1.

2.

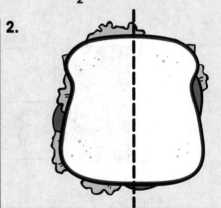

3.

4.

Exploring Fractions

This rectangle is cut into three equal parts, or **thirds.** The number of total parts is the bottom number. The number of shaded parts is the top number. $\frac{2}{3}$ of the rectangle is shaded.

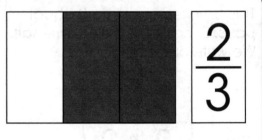

$$\frac{2}{3}$$

Study the example above. Then, write how many pieces of each shape is shaded.

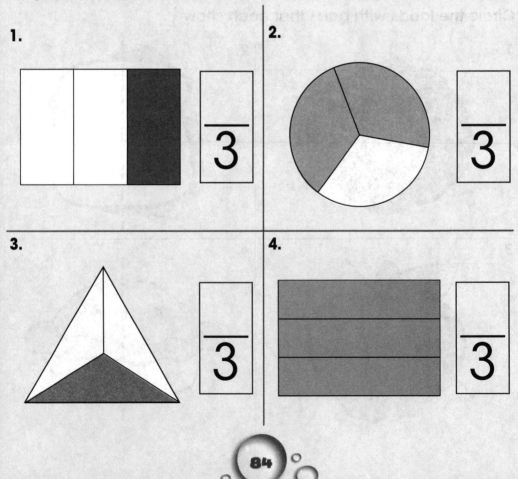

1.

$$\frac{}{3}$$

2.

$$\frac{}{3}$$

3.

$$\frac{}{3}$$

4.

$$\frac{}{3}$$

Looking for Patterns

Patterns are repeating pictures or numbers that can be predicted. This pattern is circle, square, circle, square. A circle comes next.

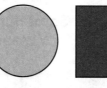

Study the example above. Then, look at each pattern below. Draw what comes next.

1. What comes next?

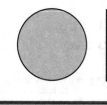

2. What comes next?

3. What comes next?

4. What comes next?

5. What comes next?

6. What comes next?

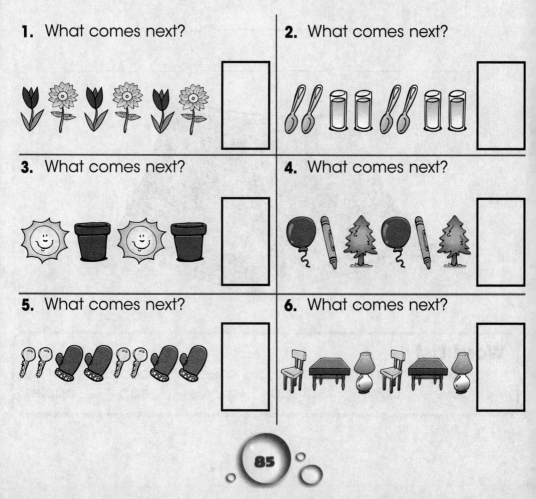

Pack These Words for Camp

Read each word in the box at the bottom of the page. Decide if it is something to eat, something to wear, or a place to live. Write it under the correct group name.

Something to Eat	Something to Wear	A Place to Live
_____	_____	_____
_____	_____	_____
_____	_____	_____
_____	_____	_____

Word List

shirt	pants	lodge	cheese	beans	tent
cave	cabin	bread	gloves	cap	apples

To the Moon

A **fact** is something that you know is true.
An **opinion** is what you believe about something.
Example: Mr. Greene is a teacher. (This is a fact.)
                 Mr. Greene is the best teacher. (This is an opinion.)

Get the rocket to the moon. Color the stars that tell a fact blue.

Earth
is a
planet.

It is fun
to ride in
a rocket.

Earth has
a moon.

The sun
is the
best star.

Stars
are
interesting.

There are
many stars
in the sky.

Earth is the
greatest
planet.

Stars are
beautiful.

The sun
gives Earth
light.

What Will Happen?

Read each passage. Read the three endings. Choose the ending that makes the most sense.

1. Jade's class was going on a trip. They were going to the zoo. A big bus came to get them.
   - **A.** They all went home.
   - **B.** They got on the bus.
   - **C.** They went out to play.

2. They rode for a long time. Then, the bus came to a stop. They were at the zoo!
   - **A.** They all got off.
   - **B.** They went to the store.
   - **C.** They got up on top of the bus.

3. They went into the zoo. They went to see the lion. He had a big mane. He had big teeth.
   - **A.** He ate a car.
   - **B.** He was not there.
   - **C.** He had a big roar.

Tanner and Andy's Clubhouse

Directions are steps for doing something. Always be sure to do each step in order. Do not skip any steps. Pay attention to key words, such as number words and color words.

Help Tanner and Andy finish building their clubhouse. Follow each step in order.

1. Draw the outline of a house.
2. Draw two square windows.
3. Write *Clubhouse* above the door.
4. Draw a rectangle around the word *Clubhouse*.
5. Color the clubhouse brown.
6. Color the door red.
7. Draw a roof.
8. Color the roof green.
9. Draw yourself near the clubhouse.

Pattern Practice

Study the example on page 85. Then, continue each pattern by drawing and coloring the next three shapes.

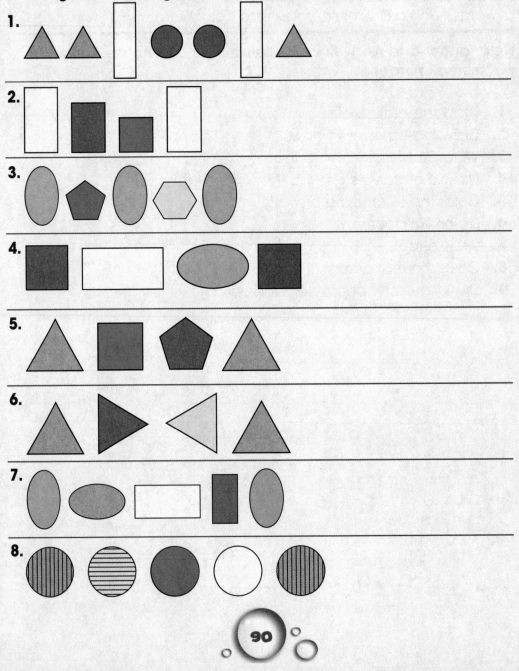

Basic Shapes

These are basic shapes.

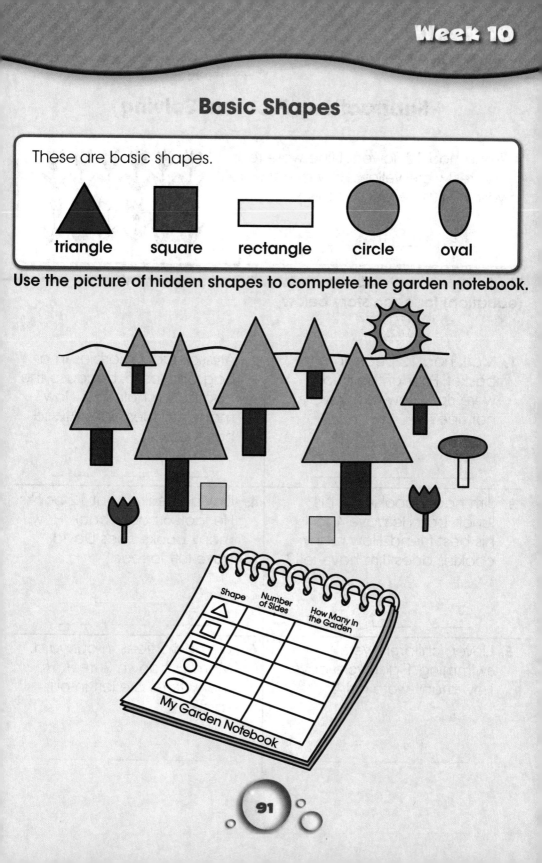

| triangle | square | rectangle | circle | oval |

Use the picture of hidden shapes to complete the garden notebook.

Shape	Number of Sides	How Many In the Garden
△		
□		
▭		
○		
⬭		

My Garden Notebook

Subtraction (Problem Solving)

Anna had 12 flowers. Nine were red.
The rest were yellow. How many were
yellow? (Three were yellow.)

$$\underline{12} - \underline{9} = \underline{3}$$

**Study the example above. Then, write a number sentence
(equation) for each story below.**

1. Mark had 12 pears in a
basket. Four of the pears
were ripe. How many were
not ripe?

___ - ___ = ___

2. Alyssa had 7 marbles in a
bag. She lost 5, because the
bag had a hole in it. How
many marbles does Alyssa
have left?

___ - ___ = ___

3. Jim had 9 cookies in his
lunch box. He gave 4 to
his best friend. How many
cookies does Jim have left?

___ - ___ = ___

4. David checked out 12 books.
He took 6 books back. How
many books does David
have left to read?

___ - ___ = ___

5. Eleven children were
swimming. Eight were boys.
How many were girls?

___ - ___ = ___

6. We had 8 trees in our yard.
Mom cut down 2 trees. How
many trees are left in our
yard?

___ - ___ = ___

Finding Missing Information

Sometimes, drawing a picture or writing a math problem can help you solve a story problem.

Write a math problem to find the answer to each question below.

1. Twelve children are playing on the swings. Seven of them are girls. How many boys are playing on the swings?

2. A family drives 14 miles to the beach. Then, they drive home. How many total miles did the family drive?

3. The farmer's horse eats 3 buckets of food each day. How many buckets of food will he eat in 2 days?

4. Brittney is 8 years old. Her brother is 5 years older. How old is Brittney's brother?

5. The cage holds 12 birds. Eight of them are black. How many are not black?

6. Eighteen children began climbing the rope. Nine made it to the top. How many children did not make it to the top?

Answer Key

Page 15: 1. cat, hat, bat, sat; **2.** Max; **3.** cap, hat, bag, bat; **4.** Answers will vary.; **5.** Answers will vary.; **6.** Picture should show Sam and Max.

Page 17: 1. B.; **2.** T, T, F, T, F, F, T; **3.** B.; **4.** A.; **5.** Big pets: horse, sheep, cow; Little pets: gerbil, hamster, mouse; **6.** Meg, Vet, pets, help, get, well, leg, mend, pep

Page 18: Words should be traced correctly.

Page 19: 1. 4; **2.** 0; **3.** 9; **4.** 11; **5.** 3; **6.** 7; **7.** 12; **8.** 8; **9.** 5

Page 20: Lines should be drawn correctly to connect bees and flowers.

Page 21: Fish from left to right: orange, red, green, yellow, blue, red, green; cars from left to right: green, red, blue, red, brown, black, brown

Page 23: 1. A.; **2.** fish, dish; ship, trip; chip, dip; pig, jig; **3.** A.; **4.** Y, Y, Y, N; **5.** Answers will vary.

Page 25: 1. B.; **2.** T, F, T, F; **3.** A.; **4. A.** man, **B.** gold, **C.** pots; **5.** A.; **6.** A.

Page 26: From left to right and top to bottom: 8, 10, 12, 14, 16, 18, 20, 22, 24, 26, 28, 30, 32, 34, 36, 38, 40, 42, 44, 46, 48, 50, 52, 54

Page 27: From left to right and top to bottom: 5, 10, 15, 20, 25, 30, 35, 40, 45, 50, 55, 60, 65, 70, 75, 80, 85, 90, 95, 100

Page 28: The dot-to-dots should connect by 10s to make a cat, an owl, and a slice of watermelon.

Page 29: 1. 9; **2.** 1; **3.** 4; **4.** 5; **5.** 3; **6.** 7; **7.** 6; **8.** 2

Page 31: 1. B.; **2.** 4, 2, 1, 3, 5; **3.** B.; **4.** Answers will vary.; **5.** B.

Page 32: 1. quick; **2.** keep; **3.** kind; **4.** sleep; **5.** run; **6.** choose

Page 33: 1. day, night; **2.** long, short; **3.** big, little; **4.** hot, cold; **5.** old, new; **6.** over, under

Page 34: 1. left group; **2.** right group; **3.** right group; **4.** right group; **5.** left group; **6.** right group; **7.** left group.; **8.** left group

Page 35: 1. left group; **2.** right group; **3.** right group; **4.** left group; **5.** left group; **6.** right group; **7.** left group; **8.** right group

Page 36: From left to right and top to bottom: >, >, <, <, >, <, <, <

Page 37: 1. 4; **2.** 6; **3.** 4; **4.** 5; Objects should be colored correctly.

Page 38: 1. My Pet Fish; **2.** A Trip to the Moon; **3.** Fun at the Pool; **4.** A Bird Adventure; **5.** I'm All Wet!; **6.** The Cat Picture; **7.** Answers will vary.

Page 39:

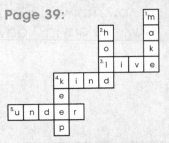

Page 40: 1. 2, 3, 1; **2.** 2, 1, 3; **3.** 3, 2, 1; **4.** 2, 3, 1

Page 41: 1. Wheels make things easy to move.; **2.** People had to move things without wheels.

94